DATE DUE

VIOLIN
AND STRINGED INSTRUMENTS

CONTENTS

Designed and produced by
Aladdin Books Ltd

First published in
the United States in 1993
Gloucester Press
95 Madison Avenue
New York, N.Y. 10016

Printed in Belgium

Music copyright © Philippa Bunting
1992
Series designer: David West
Design: Andy Wilkinson
Editor: Jen Green
Picture researcher: Emma Krikler
Illustrators: Ron Hayward, David West

Library of Congress
Cataloging-in-Publication Data

Hunka, Alison.
    Violin and stringed instruments /
by Alison Hunka and Philippa
Bunting.
        p.   cm. -- (Young musician
plays)
    Includes index.
    ISBN 0-531-17424-7
    1. Violin--Instruction and study--
Juvenile.   [1. Violin--Instruction
and study.]   I. Bunting, Philippa.
II. Title.   III. Series.
MT760.H86   1993
787.2--dc20   93-20635
                                CIP
                            AC MN

YOUNG MUSICIAN PLAYS

VIOLIN
AND STRINGED INSTRUMENTS

ALISON HUNKA
AND
PHILIPPA BUNTING

GLOUCESTER PRESS
NEW YORK • CHICAGO • LONDON • TORONTO • SYDNEY

INTRODUCTION

The violin is one of the best loved of all musical instruments. The beauty of its shape is matched by a beauty of tone. The violin is a member of the family of stringed instruments. It is capable of a wide range of musical expression: the sound of the violin can be almost as varied and as moving as the human voice.

When a violin string is plucked or bowed it starts to vibrate. These vibrations pass through the bridge to the soundpost inside the violin. The sound is then amplified throughout the hollow inner chamber, and escapes through the f-shaped sound holes in the belly.

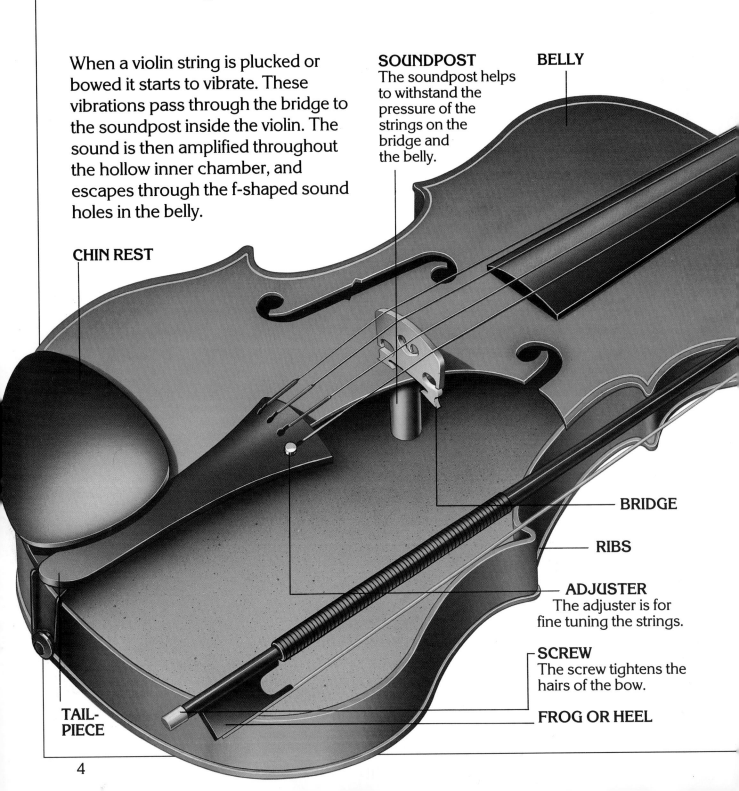

SOUNDPOST
The soundpost helps to withstand the pressure of the strings on the bridge and the belly.

BELLY

CHIN REST

BRIDGE

RIBS

ADJUSTER
The adjuster is for fine tuning the strings.

SCREW
The screw tightens the hairs of the bow.

TAIL-PIECE

FROG OR HEEL

PARTS OF THE VIOLIN AND BOW

The violin is made up of about 85 separate parts, each of which has an important rôle to play in the production of sound.

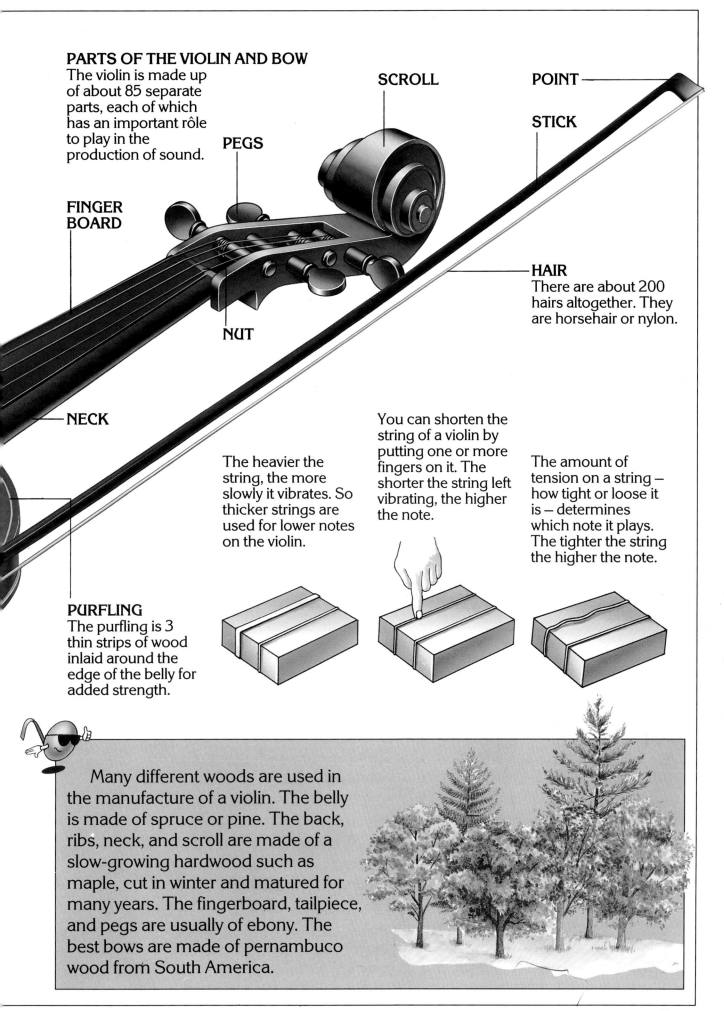

SCROLL

POINT

STICK

PEGS

FINGER BOARD

NUT

NECK

HAIR
There are about 200 hairs altogether. They are horsehair or nylon.

The heavier the string, the more slowly it vibrates. So thicker strings are used for lower notes on the violin.

You can shorten the string of a violin by putting one or more fingers on it. The shorter the string left vibrating, the higher the note.

The amount of tension on a string – how tight or loose it is – determines which note it plays. The tighter the string the higher the note.

PURFLING
The purfling is 3 thin strips of wood inlaid around the edge of the belly for added strength.

Many different woods are used in the manufacture of a violin. The belly is made of spruce or pine. The back, ribs, neck, and scroll are made of a slow-growing hardwood such as maple, cut in winter and matured for many years. The fingerboard, tailpiece, and pegs are usually of ebony. The best bows are made of pernambuco wood from South America.

5

GETTING TO KNOW THE VIOLIN

Before you begin to play, you must find a way of holding your violin that feels comfortable and natural. Ideally your violin should feel part of you. You should be able to hold it just tightly enough to keep it from slipping, but not so tightly that your shoulder and neck muscles tense up. Being relaxed when you play will make everything much easier.

GETTING READY TO PLAY

Stand with your feet shoulder-width apart. Hold the back of the violin against your stomach, with your left hand around the neck and your right hand under the chin rest. Now stretch your arms out to the left, turn the violin and place it on your left shoulder. Let the instrument lie along your left collar-bone. Turn your head to look toward the scroll, and the side of your jaw will fall naturally onto the chin rest.

SITTING POSITION

When violinists have to play for long periods of time, for example in an orchestra, they usually play sitting down. This is less tiring on the legs, but makes it harder to maintain a comfortable violin position. Standing up allows the player greater freedom of movement, so violinists usually stand up when they practice or play solos. If you do have to play sitting down, both of your feet should be flat on the floor. Your knees should be apart and your back should be straight but not stiff. Hold your violin as you would if you were standing.

HOLDING YOUR VIOLIN

The violin can be held without any help from the left hand – try it and see! However, the left hand can provide some useful support. Bring your left thumb up to the place where the neck meets the body of the violin and let your fingers rest above the strings.

PLUCKING

You are now ready to try plucking. Gently tug at one of the strings with the first finger of your right hand, and let go. Pluck the string about 1in (2 cm) from the end of the fingerboard. Bring your hand around in a circle, and come back to pluck a different string.

FIRST POSITIONS

In its early days, the violin was held against the player's chest with the thumb under the frog of the bow. Later the violin was held loosely under the chin, without allowing the head to rest on the instrument (there were no chin rests in those days). The player's elbow was held against his or her side. Both positions are still used by some contemporary folk musicians. The position we use today allows us to play more difficult music. Early bows were shaped like an archer's bow, with the wood bent outward from the hair rather than toward it.

MAKING A START

On the previous page you got to know your violin a little, and heard some of the sounds it can make. Now you are ready to learn more about what those sounds are, and how they can be put together to make music. Each of the violin's four strings is tuned to a particular note. The strings are named after these notes.

THE OPEN STRINGS

Starting with the lowest in pitch, the four open strings are G, D, A, and E. Pluck them in turn and say their names. Now try and sing the same notes. Can you hear how different the sounds are? Each string has its own individual character, like a person, and violinists make use of this to bring out the character of the music.

G   D   A   E

TUNING THE VIOLIN

Tuning is something you may need help with at first, as the strings need to be

You can also buy sets of pitch pipes, with a note for each string.

at exactly the right tension and pitch for you to be able to play the right notes. You can tune the strings to a piano or to a tuning fork, which is more reliable. To change the pitch of a string you use the tuning pegs, or adjusters if you have them.

PLUCKING PRACTICE

Here is a simple tune for you to pluck. It will help you to get to know the four open strings. Play the large letters as long notes and the small letters as short notes. Try this tune line by line. Listen to the notes as you play them. Then try playing the piece all the way through, with the long and short notes making the right rhythm.

A D A D   GGGG D D

A E AA E   EEEE A A

D AA DD D   G GG D D

A E A E   AAAA D D

WHAT DID YOU HAVE FOR BREAKFAST?

Now try inventing, or improvising, music for yourself. In the last piece, the long and short notes made up a rhythm. Make up your own rhythm now, by saying your name and address aloud. You could also try saying what you had for breakfast.

Now pluck along as you speak, to make a musical picture of the rhythm of the words. Choose different strings to suit the different things you are saying. You could even try having a conversation between two strings!

HOW STRINGS ARE MADE

All violin strings used to be made from sheepgut. Then it was discovered  that winding aluminum or silver thread around the gut meant that strings could be made stronger and thinner. Now nylon or plastic is often used instead of gut for the central core, and the strings are wound with aluminum or copper wire. The material from which the string is made affects the quality of the sound it produces.

9

READING THE NOTES

In written music, notes are shown as dots on a set of five lines called a staff. The higher the notes appear on the staff, the higher they are in pitch. Being able to read musical notation means that you can play music written by other people.

NAMING THE NOTES

Musical notes are named after the letters of the alphabet, from A to G. After G the letters begin again. In the diagram on the right, the open strings of your violin are represented in musical notation, and as notes on the keyboard. Open string D is just below the five lines of the staff. The note above, on the lowest line of the staff, is E. The note in the space above is F, the note on the next line is G, and then comes open string A. All the open strings appear in spaces.

The treble clef symbol (below) indicates the pitch range of the notes for the violin.

G   D   A   E

LEDGER LINES

The pitch of a note means how high or low the note is. Notes like open string G are pitched too high or low to fit on the staff. Little extra lines, like steps on a ladder, reach up or down to them. These are known as ledger lines.

10

OPEN STRING PRACTICE

Now that you know what the open strings of your violin look like in notation, you are ready to practice reading them. All the notes below are the same length. You'll see that the written notes form a visual image of the notes you hear as you play. The higher the notes appear on the staff, the higher the sound you hear.

As you read the music, look ahead at the notes that come next. As you play one note you should know what the next one is, so that your hand leaves the string traveling in the right direction for the next note. The vertical lines below are bar lines. They organize the music into easy-to-read units called bars or measures.

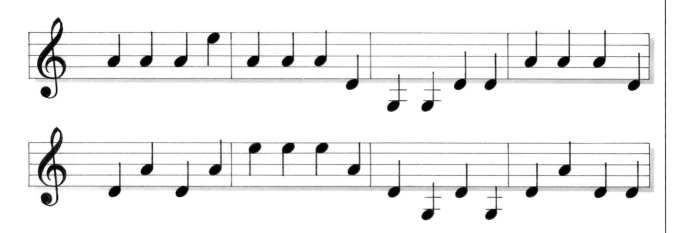

THE FIRST VIOLINS

The violin-like instrument in this medieval French miniature is a *lyra de bracchia*, an ancestor of the violin. When the violin first appeared in the 16th century, it was mainly used as an instrument to play music at dances and weddings, and was not regarded very highly. More popular with composers and musicians was the family of viols. These stringed instruments were made in various sizes, and were designed to be played together in groups or consorts. They were held between the knees, and played with a bow. They had frets to guide the fingers of the left hand, as guitars do today. By the 18th century viols had been replaced by the violin and its family of instruments.

ADDING THE BEAT

The beat of a piece of music is like the ticking of a clock or the pulse of a metronome. Most of the time it stays regular, but the rhythm – the pattern of long and short notes – varies within this basic beat. On this page you can see how long and short notes look when they are written down.

One
whole note
=
two
half notes
=
four
quarter notes
=
eight
eighth notes

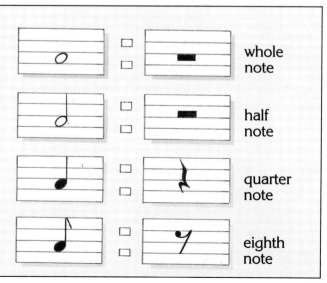

Notes of different time values are written in different ways. Each of the rows shown above uses up the same amount of time in the music.

The whole note is the longest single note here. It takes up the same space in time as two half notes, four quarter notes, and eight eighth notes.

RESTS

In music, the silence between notes is just as important as the notes you play. In written music, silence is represented by symbols called rests. Different symbols represent silences of different time values, which correspond to the notes above. When you come to a rest in musical notation, try to think of it as a silent note, and remember to give it its full time value.

𝅝	▯	whole note
𝅗𝅥	▯	half note
♩	♩	quarter note
♪	𝄾	eighth note

Different pieces of music have different numbers of beats in a bar. The time signature at the beginning of the music tells you about this. The bottom number tells you what note forms the basic beat. In all the examples which appear above, it is a quarter note beat.

The top number tells you how many beats there are in a bar. The first example above, 2/4 time, has two quarter notes to the bar, or the equivalent made up of notes of other time values. 3/4 time has three, and 4/4 time four quarter notes to the bar. Try out these examples.

TRADITIONAL SKILLS
The violin plays a major part in the Eastern European musical tradition. Gypsy violinists (right) are famous for their skillful playing and the mournful quality of much of their music. The fiddle has also been the most popular folk instrument in North America for a long time; on the opposite page you can see two early American musicians. In the United States, the fiddle has a repertoire of over 1,000 tunes, and some fiddlers are said to know more than 400 from memory.

DOWN TO BUSINESS

You are now familiar with the open strings. On this page you can find out how to sound some of the notes in between. These notes are made by placing the fingers of your left hand on the strings in different positions.

NUT

1

2

3

For playing the violin the fingers of your left hand are numbered as shown.

3
2
1

Put your fingers on the strings as shown. Your thumb, helping to support the violin, touches the neck opposite your first and second fingers.

Putting your finger on the violin string shortens the length of the string that vibrates, and produces a higher note. The gap between the nut and the first finger is the same as the gap between fingers 1 and 2 (a whole step); the gap between fingers 2 and 3 is half that distance (a half step).

Pluck open string D with your left hand in place ready for the next note.

Put your left index finger down. Pluck the string to sound the note E.

Put your second finger down a little way from the first. This note is F sharp.

Add your third finger so that it touches your second. This note is G.

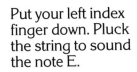
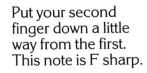

D STRING PRACTICE

This tune uses all the notes you have learned on the D string. Notice that the fingering has been marked over the notes to help you. Try plucking this exercise now. Then come back to it later and play it with the bow.

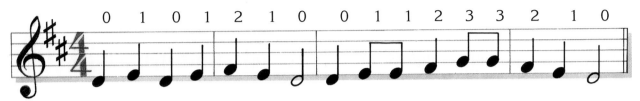

TRYING OUT THE A STRING

The finger pattern for the D string – a large gap between the nut and the first finger and between fingers 1 and 2, and half the distance between fingers 2 and 3 – works for the other strings too. Now try the pattern on the A string.

D MAJOR

Putting all these notes together, you can play your first scale, the scale of D major. The symbols in the "key signature" by the treble clef are sharps. Here sharps appear on the notes F and C, indicating the key of D major.

ANTONIO VIVALDI

Antonio Vivaldi (1678–1741) was one of the most important and prolific composers for the violin. He lived in Venice, and entered the priesthood at 15. He was nicknamed "the red priest" because of his red hair. Vivaldi wrote nearly 400 concertos for the violin. A concerto is a composition for a solo instrument and orchestra. Vivaldi's most famous work is *The Four Seasons*, a set of four concertos, one for each season of the year.

15

TAKING UP THE BOW

A violin without a bow is only really half an instrument. The bow releases the violin's "voice." *Pizzicato* (plucking) is a useful effect in music, but the bow unlocks the violin's full range of expression. The first step is to become as comfortable with the bow as you are now with the violin itself.

HOLDING THE BOW

Practicing your bowhold with a pencil first is a good idea. Make a circle with your right thumb and two middle fingers. Your thumb should be opposite your fingers, so that you can feel your thumbnail. Now take up your bow in the same way, holding it at the frog end. Your thumb should rest under the stick of the bow opposite your middle fingers. Your index finger now joins the middle two over the stick, with space between each finger. The tip of your little finger balances on top of the stick.

Place your bow on a string, with the frog end about ½ inch from the bridge.

Draw the bow slowly down toward the point and back again. As your bow hand gets further away from the violin, guide your bow so that it remains parallel to the bridge. Try bowing each string in turn without touching any of the other strings.

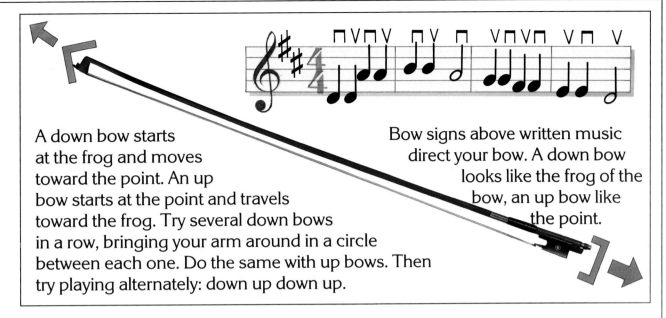

A down bow starts at the frog and moves toward the point. An up bow starts at the point and travels toward the frog. Try several down bows in a row, bringing your arm around in a circle between each one. Do the same with up bows. Then try playing alternately: down up down up.

Bow signs above written music direct your bow. A down bow looks like the frog of the bow, an up bow like the point.

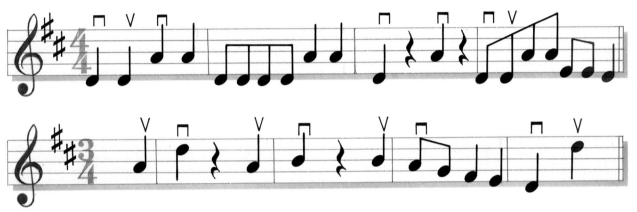

A down bow is often used on heavier beats, such as the first beat of the bar. An up bow is used on lighter beats.

Use the rests in the first piece above to make a circle with the bow, so that you are ready for the next down bow.

CARING FOR VIOLIN AND BOW

Like any musical instrument, your violin and bow need to be well cared for. Don't put your violin next to a radiator, or leave it outside overnight; if it gets too hot or cold the wood may crack. Rosin your bow regularly, but never touch the hairs of the bow with your fingers. When you finish playing, loosen your bow and wipe your violin with a soft cloth to remove old rosin. Stock your violin case with spare strings and rosin. Last but not least – keep your fingernails short!

SMOOTHING OUT THE NOTES

You can change the sound the violin makes by varying the way you draw the bow across the strings. Experiment with the speed of bow, and with the amount of weight you put on the string. Bowing close to the bridge produces a different sound. Now you are ready to try playing more than one note in each bow. This technique is called a slur.

WHAT IS A SLUR?

Singers often have one word to sing on each note. When they have one word to sing over many notes, they spread the word over all the notes in a slur. A violinist uses his or her bow to create a similar effect. You can also use slurs to vary the way you play a musical sentence, or phrase.

ONE BOW FOR MANY NOTES

So far you have learned to play with one bow to each note, so that the note and the direction of the bow change at the same time. In a slur, the bow continues to travel in the same direction as the note changes. In one bow you can sound a number of different notes.

PRACTICING SLURS

To play slurs you need to be able to do two things at once. Although they are performing separate activities, the movements of your two hands need to be coordinated, so that they work in time with each other. This is an important skill in violin playing. Practice it by putting one finger down on the A string. Start a down bow. Halfway through the bow, take your finger off. The bow should carry on smoothly, and should not jerk when the note changes. Do the same on an up bow. The noise you produce may sound like an ambulance siren!

Slurs can be between notes on the same string, or on different strings. In the second of these exercises, use your right elbow, not just your hand, to lead you from one string to the other. Then try the piece below.

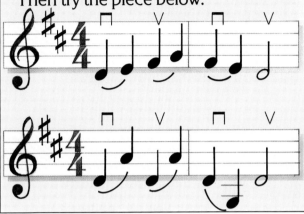

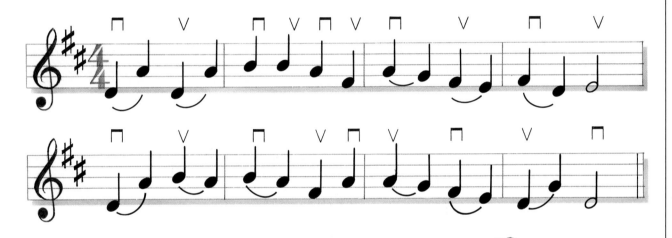

ANTONIO STRADIVARI

Antonio Stradivari (1644–1737) is generally acknowledged to be the greatest violin maker of all time. He worked in the Italian town of Cremona, and made over 1,000 instruments during the course of his career. Of these about 600 survive now, some of which are in museums. Many of Stradivari's instruments have been given individual names – two of his finest violins are called the "Alard" and the "Messiah."

MOVING ON

This page shows you how to play the other notes you can make using the simple finger pattern you learned on pages 14–15. With these notes you will be able to play two more scales: A major and G major. Once you feel sure of these notes, try picking out some simple tunes from memory – or make some up yourself!

SCALE OF A MAJOR

The scale of A major uses the same finger pattern as the scale of D major, but it is played on the A and E strings. Scales are patterns of large and small gaps (whole steps and half steps).

These gaps, or intervals, stay the same whatever note you start on. To preserve the pattern, the scale of A major has three sharps: F, C, and G. You can see them in the key signature.

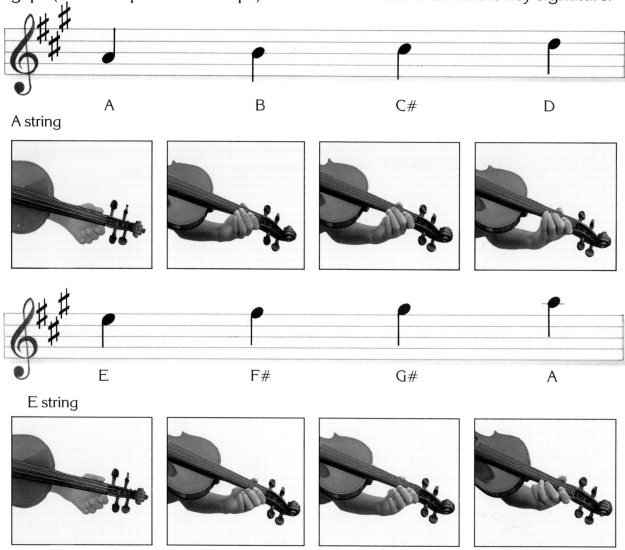

SCALE OF G MAJOR

The scale of G major uses the same finger pattern as the other two scales you have learned, but it is played on the G and D strings. G major has one sharp, F, in the key signature. Use one long bow to each note.

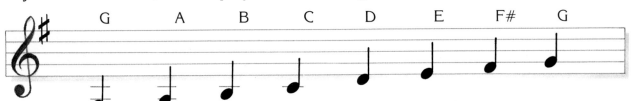

G A B C D E F# G

GOOD AND BAD HABITS

Bad habits are easy to pick up and very hard to unlearn later. This is particularly true of playing the violin, because there are so many things going on at once that it is hard to keep track of them all! Some of the basic rules are as follows:

Don't do anything that makes you tense, or anything that hurts.
Keep your shoulders down and keep them loose.
Don't tighten the muscles in your neck when you get to a part of the music that you find difficult.
Stay as relaxed as possible. You'll find that you play much better, and are able to enjoy it more!

How many bad habits can you spot in this photo?

NICCOLÒ PAGANINI

Paganini (1782–1840) was the greatest violin player of his day. He wrote his own music to display his expertise. His musical genius and eccentric appearance led to rumors that he had made a pact with the devil to enhance his playing. His "Napoleon" sonata is played on the G string alone.

FIRST MELODIES

By now you may be starting to pick out some of the tunes you know from memory. This page gives you an opportunity to practice playing written music. Using everything you have learned, try out these melodies; as you play, remember to listen carefully to check that you are playing in tune, and producing a good sound.

THE LONESOME FIDDLER

Before you begin to play, study the music. Look at the key signature and the time signature. "The Lonesome Fiddler" is in 4/4 time, with four quarter notes to the bar.

Try clapping the rhythm of the piece before you start. As you play, think about the intervals between the notes, not just where you are going to put each finger. This will help you to play in tune. Don't start moving the bow until your fingers are in the right place – as you get more experienced at playing you will get quicker at doing this. Finally, enjoy playing the music – that's what it's all about!

RAINBOW WALTZ

"The Rainbow Waltz," like all waltzes, is in 3/4 time, with three quarter notes to the bar. Each piece of music has its own character, which you must try to bring out.

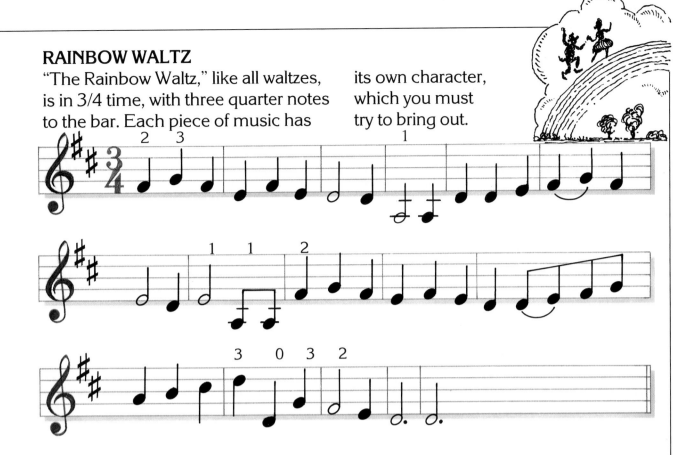

PLAYING WITH OTHERS

Many people learn to play the violin in a group. This is one of the best ways to learn, because you hear other people play and get used to playing with them. There are many methods for learning in groups. If you have the chance, join a string group or an orchestra. You may make new friends!

PLAYING TOGETHER

Playing with other people is one of the most exciting and rewarding aspects of learning an instrument. Playing with just one other person is a good place to start. A piece of music for two people to play is called a duet. One written especially for you appears below. It is written in the key of D major, with F sharp and C sharp in the key signature.

MUSIC BOX

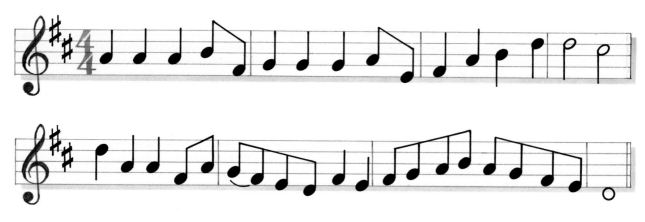

FIRST VIOLIN

In order to play successfully with someone else, you need to know your own part well. Start by trying the first violin part, which carries the melody. Then see if you can also play the second violin part, which is the accompaniment. Both parts are equally important! Finally, try playing this duet with a friend or with your teacher. When you put the two parts together, make sure both players start and finish at exactly the same time!

THE RANGE OF THE VIOLIN

The full range of the violin extends over four octaves (the scales you have learned so far were one octave scales). Some very difficult music uses the full range of the instrument, from one end of the fingerboard to the other. With work, there is no reason why you should not be able to play music like this in time, although pieces that are hard to play are not always the most rewarding musically!

SECOND VIOLIN

The second violin part is more complicated than the first, as it moves faster and crosses strings more often. When you play it with a partner, listen to make sure that the rhythm of your accompaniment fits with the tune. Give the rests their full value and listen to what the first violin is playing.

MUSIC BOX

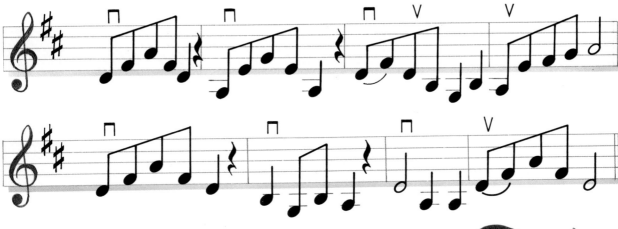

JAZZ VIOLIN

The violin can be used to great effect in jazz. This music is not written down, but is improvised (made up) by the players as they go along. Two of the most famous jazz violinists were Stephane Grapelli and Joe Venuti, both of whom often played in duos with guitarists. Nigel Kennedy is a classically trained violinist who also plays jazz.

THE WORLD OF THE VIOLIN

The variety of musical effects possible on the violin makes it one of the most popular of all musical instruments. All over the world, you will find people playing violins or similar kinds of musical instruments. The versatility of the violin makes it suitable for playing many different styles of music.

THE ORCHESTRA

There are more violins in the orchestra than any other instrument. They are divided into first and second violin sections. The first violins often play the melody, and the second violins the accompaniment, as in the duet on the previous page. Two players share each music stand, and all the players in a section play the same music. Violinists in an orchestra blend in their individual sound with the other violins in their section. In this way, a violin section sounds like one great instrument.

THE CONCERTMASTER

The leader of a section sits at the front. All the other players follow what he or she does. The leader of the first violins is also concertmaster of the orchestra. This tradition dates back to the time when orchestras were smaller and didn't have conductors. The concertmaster directed the orchestra and played at the same time.

STREET MUSIC

The violin is light and portable. As a solo instrument, the music it produces is expressive and appealing. These qualities make it a good instrument for street music. You may have seen violinists playing in subway stations or in the open air, collecting money in a hat or in a violin case.

VIOLIN AND PIANO

When a violinist plays in a duo with one other musician, it is most often with a pianist. There is a huge repertoire of music written for this combination of instruments. In some of this music both instruments are equally important, in some the piano accompanies the violin.

STRING QUARTET

A quartet is a group of four musicians. A string quartet has two violins in it, which play different parts. The other instruments are viola and cello. As in an orchestra, the first violin is the leader of the group. Many composers wrote some of their most wonderful music for string quartet.

STRING FAMILY

The violin is the smallest member of the string family, and the highest in pitch. It was also the first to be invented. The violin's immediate relatives – the viola, cello, and double bass – can also be either bowed or plucked. As the body of the instrument gets bigger, so its range of notes becomes lower.

VIOLA, CELLO, AND DOUBLE BASS
The viola (below) is slightly bigger than the violin, and is held in the same way. The cello (right) is even bigger, and is played sitting down. The instrument is held between the player's knees, and rests on an endpin or spike. Largest and deepest is the double bass (far right), which has the same strings as the violin, but in the reverse order. Bass players play sitting on a high stool, or standing up.

THE CONCERT HARP

The other member of the string family with a regular place in the symphony orchestra is the concert harp. Each string of the harp produces one note when plucked; each of these notes can be lowered or raised half a tone by means of pedals. The characteristic sound of the harp makes it instantly recognizable, even when the whole orchestra is playing. Also related are the guitar and the zither, which is a folk instrument.

THE STRINGS IN THE ORCHESTRA

The stringed instruments form the mainstay of the modern Western symphony or chamber orchestra. Together the strings cover a range of over seven octaves. It is even possible to have an orchestra made up solely of string players – a string orchestra. The variety of effects possible with stringed instruments, such as *pizzicato* (see page 16) makes them very popular with composers.

GEOGRAPHY OF THE ORCHESTRA

The diagram below shows how a symphony orchestra is usually laid out. The stringed instruments are spread across the front of the platform in a semicircle, ranging from the violins on the left to the double basses on the far right. The conductor stands at the front, surrounded by string players. If the piece is a concerto, the soloist stands or sits next to the conductor.

POSITIONS OF THE STRINGS

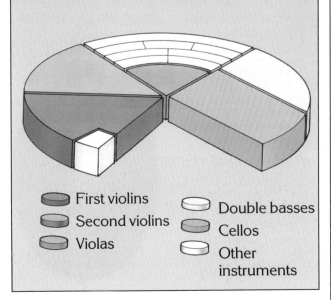

First violins

Second violins

Violas

Double basses

Cellos

Other instruments

ALTO AND BASS CLEFS

The lower stringed instruments read music written in different clefs, although both the viola and the cello sometimes use the treble clef. The viola usually plays music written in the alto clef (below left) and the cello uses the bass clef (right). So does the double bass, but its notes sound an octave lower than written.

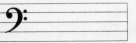

COMPOSERS AND PERFORMERS

Violins were first made during the Renaissance period. The instrument quickly became popular, and composers were writing music for it by the late 17th century. As players' skill (technique) became more advanced, so violin music became more difficult. Recently the violin has come to be used in jazz and pop as well as in classical music.

Handel

The violin began to take its present-day form in the early 16th century. By the beginning of the 17th century, the great Cremonese violin-making families of Stradivari, Guarneri, and Amati were making violins that are still considered to be the best in the world.

Originally the violin was used mainly for popular dance music. The first composer to write specifically for it was **Corelli** (1653–1713), a celebrated violinist and teacher. Even the hardest pieces he wrote seem quite easy by modern technical standards. **Handel** (1685–1759) wrote many beautiful violin sonatas.

Tartini (1692–1770) was another baroque violinist-composer. His famous "Devil's Trill" sonata is one of the first virtuoso violin pieces. He claimed that the devil had shown him how to play it in a dream.

Bach (1685–1750) wrote sonatas, suites, and partitas for solo violin and for solo cello. The famous cellist Pablo Casals used to play one every day before breakfast, because he considered them to be the foundation

Mozart

of all great music.

In the classical era, the violin came to play an important role in orchestral and chamber music. It also featured as a solo instrument in concertos.

Mozart (1756–1791) spent much of his childhood on tour as a child prodigy. He wrote his five violin concertos in one year, when he was 19. He also wrote much chamber music that includes the violin.

Beethoven (1770–1827) also wrote sonatas. His violin concerto, a dramatic piece, opens with four ominous drumbeats.

Mendelssohn

The virtuoso violin concerto became a very popular form in the course of the 19th century. **Mendelssohn** (1809–1847) and **Bruch** (1838–1920) wrote two of the most popular violin concertos of all time. When **Brahms** (1833–1897) wrote his violin concerto it was first thought to be unplayable. It was called a concerto not for but against the violin.

Other great violin concertos include those by **Tchaikovsky**, **Sibelius**, **Elgar** and **Dvorak**.

The 19th century also saw the growth

Grapelli

of salon concerts, often given in the houses of rich patrons, for which violinists wrote their own music. Some such violinist-composers were **Wieniawski**, **Sarasate**, and **Kreisler**, who pretended some of his pieces were by little-known baroque composers. The violin came to be seen as a "respectable" instrument for women to play through the performances of such female virtuosi as Wilma Norman-Neruda and Erica Morini.

Perhaps the greatest single influence on the violin world since Paganini, **Heifetz** is known for the technical brilliance of his performances, and for the speed at which he played some pieces! The more complex music of the twentieth century brought with it new challenges for the violinist. **Berg**

Menuhin

(1885–1935) wrote his violin concerto in memory of a young girl. It begins with just the four open strings. The music of **Bartók** (1881–1945) is based on Hungarian and Gypsy folk music, which is particularly clear in his writing for the violin. Russian composers **Stravinsky** (1882–

Kyung-Wha Chung

1971), and **Shostakovich** (1906–1975) both wrote one violin concerto. **Prokofiev** (1891–1953) wrote two concertos.

The tradition of the violin virtuoso who dazzles with his or her technical brilliance is no less alive than it was a hundred years ago. The violin is also being used again, as it was originally, as a popular instrument. Outstanding players include **Kyung-Wha Chung**, **Nigel Kennedy**, **Stephane Grapelli**, **Yehudi Menuhin**, **Nathan Milstein**, **David Oistrakh**, and **Itzhak Perlman**.

GLOSSARY

arco playing with the bow, as distinct from *pizzicato* (see below).

chamber music music for small groups of players, once designed to be played in private homes.

dynamics commands telling you how loud or soft to play.

flat note lowered in pitch by a half step.

improvisation when the players make up the music as they go along. Jazz is mostly improvised music.

interval the distance in pitch between two notes. The interval between your strings is called a perfect fifth.

key signature sometimes contains one or more sharps or flats, to indicate which key to play in. For example, the key of A major has three sharps.

mute a device which stops the bridge from passing on the vibrations efficiently, and so quiets the sound of the violin.

octave an interval of eight notes. Two notes an octave apart have the same letter name.

pizzicato plucking

scale taken from the Italian word for "step." Scales are fixed patterns of notes on which much music is based.

sharp note that is raised in pitch by a half step.

technique the mechanical aspect of violin playing, and the basis for advanced music making.

tutti the whole orchestra playing together, without the soloist.

virtuoso a player with astounding technical ability; also, the kind of music that enables the player to show off that technique!

INDEX

Photocredits
Cover and pages 4-5, 6 both, 7 top left and right, 8, 9, 10, 14 all, 16 both, 17, 18 all, 20, 21 right, 23, 24 and 28 all: Roger Vlitos; pages 7 bottom, 11, 25

top, 27 middle, 30 top left and right and 30 bottom left: Mary Evans Picture Library; pages 12, 22, 25 bottom and 31 bottom: Topham Picture Source;

pages 13, 15, 19 and 21 left: Hulton Picture Company; pages 26 top, 27 top and 29: British Broadcasting Corporation; page 26 bottom: J. Allan

Cash Photolibrary; pages 27 bottom and 30 bottom right: Frank Spooner Pictures; page 31 top: Popperfoto.